Whites and Blacks; or, The Question Settled

Whites and Blacks,

— OR —

THE QUESTION SETTLED.

— — — —

—— BY ——

HON. C. H. J. TAYLOR,

Attorney at Law, and Late United States Minister Resident and Consul-General to Liberia.

PRICE, 25 CENTS.

ATLANTA, GEORGIA
JAS. P. HARRISON & CO., PRINTERS
1889

Yours for God and my Country,

C. H. J. TAYLOR.

FROM A FRIEND

The writer of this pamphlet is a remarkable man. He has held as many honorable positions as any man of his race in the United States. Leading his college class, graduating with honor, studying law, teaching school, admitted to the bar of the lowest courts, battling his way into the Supreme Court of the United States, deputy district attorney in an Indiana district, lecturer under the auspices of lyceums, Chairman of State Conventions, corporation attorney of Kansas City, Kansas, publisher and editor of newspapers, contributor to magazines, Secretary of Colored State Central Committees, leading and controlling spirit in the only Negro National Democratic Convention, United States Minister and Consul-General to Liberia under the administration of President Cleveland, resigned for his own free will of another paying $5,000 dollars a year, agent for the Virginia Normal and Collegiate Institute, elected from Kansas as a representative from the State at large to the Democratic National Convention of 1888, making eloquent speeches for his party which gained alike the admiration of friend and foe in New York, St. Louis, Louisiana, Missouri, Wichita and Leavenworth, Kansas, as well as in Ohio, Indiana and Iowa, chaining audiences of thousands in rapt attention by his oratory. Still a young man, being only thirty-three years old, he is as vigorous as ever, refusing to consider what is popular but being governed by what he believes to be right, sinking self in his love for his people and his country. Respected by every judge and lawyer of his acquaintance, he with modesty though surrounded by compliments and covered with praise that would ruin a weaker man, continues to practice his chosen profession, the law. His success in this respect has been the talk of the whole town. Following men of his race who had been here and conducted themselves in such a manner as to cause them to be censured on every hand, it was hardly expected that he could succeed, but he has. A number of the most prominent members of the bar in Atlanta have tried cases in which he appeared as associate counsel. Many of them have met him as a legal opponent in causes, and have admitted his splendid ability and respectful deportment. Mr. Taylor has proven that any gentleman without regard to color can live in Atlanta and be as well respected as in Boston or the most Northern city. He has published from time to time many articles of interest during his stay in Atlanta in the *Constitution* and other papers of the State. He has been kindly mentioned by all of them and we are sure that writings sent out by such a man will always find a host of deeply interested readers. The book is written in the popular style and ought to be enjoyed by all.

INTRODUCTION.

To my fellow-citizens, of every race and creed, this little pamphlet is respectfully addressed. I beg you to take it, read it, and think about what is said in its pages. This is the age of *book writing*. Oratory is at a discount. Men now, instead of attending the meetings where eminent and eloquent persons are to speak, engage their time at other work, relying confidently on the morning paper bringing to the breakfast table a full report of what was said.

I have decided to call this talk WHITES AND BLACKS, OR THE QUESTION SETTLED. In order to fully and intelligently present the views herein contained, certain divisions have been made. The talk is classified, or treated under seven different "Captions" or "Titles." Since the subject must be treated, words shall not be minced. The truth shall be told, not for the purpose of giving offense, but in order to save, or, at least, help in that direction.

This is no time to consider *what is policy, or what will suit public sentiment.* The only rule by which these views are governed is the rule of right and justice, as seen through the spectacles of Christianity. Somewhere in the book, I firmly believe, will be found the remedy for the settlement of "the race question." Read every word, read every sentence, remembering always that the intention and sole desire of the author is to do good, and not to gain any honor or glory from this effort. To God belongs all honor, glory and praise. If anything is said herein which you consider out of place, or ill-advised, remember the motive and continue to read the little book until it is entirely yours. Then make up your verdict. I have tried to avoid the use of large words, and to refrain from rhetorical word-picturing, in order to gain your favor, believing that if I attempted to show forth extraordinary learning, your *critical reading* of this message would cause you to be impressed differently from the way it is intended. You will find that what is here said is a plain statement of facts, by a very plain man. A man who cares more to stand well in the presence of God and his conscience than before any other tribunal. My aim is to serve the public. To serve my God, my country and my people, is the reason why I send these LEAVES to you. I am sure you will read THE MESSAGE in the spirit of fairness.

Yours for God and my country,

C. H. J. TAYLOR.

ATLANTA, GA., December, 1889.

TABLE OF CONTENTS.

WHITES AND BLACKS,

—OR—

THE QUESTION SETTLED.

- -- -

CHAPTER I

THE NEGRO AND THE WHITE MAN AS MASTER AND SLAVE.

Slavery arose at an early period of the world's history, out of the accident of capture in war. It was found by savages more profitable to make slaves out of prisoners of war than to kill them. The history of all the oriental nations, including the Jews, shows that they had their slaves. Reading the Homeric poems, passages are often found testifying that he who was made a prisoner was also made a slave. Aristotle defended the institution. So did Plato, he only asking that no Greek should be so placed. In fact all of the Greek philosophers refused to believe the holding of one's fellowman in bondage wrong, on the score of morals. Aristotle declared that the institution was just and right, on the ground of a diversity of race, dividing mankind into the free and the bond by nature. The civilized world denies the doctrines of these ancient minds, as witnessed by acts of manumission wherever Christianity is known. Let no man think that American slavery was the first, the only or even the most severe. By this I would not be guilty of apologizing for its presence in this country or for those men, among the many who held slaves, who so wickedly abused that institution. But duty compels the statement which is now made: *Others than Negroes have been slaves.* Others than Negroes have suffered the extreme and brutal affliction which often repaid the obedient service of those poor individuals who happened

to be under the "ban." Such were the Helots in Sparta,
the Penestae in Thessaly, the Bithynians at Byzantium
and the Thracians of Thrace. Grecian history teaches
that these were slaves, that these were freed, and that
these became the equals, in every respect, of those who
once held them in bondage. Can our slavery be compared with theirs? The Helots, the Penestae and the
Bithynians, though being the property and at the dis-
posal of their owners, could not be sold out of the
country or separated from their families, and were even
capable of acquiring property. It is said that numbers
of them were encouraged in cultivating their intellects,
especially where proven to have natural ability. None
of these slaves were Negroes. The Thracian parents
who sold their children into slavery were not of the
Hamitic line. Strabo declares that notwithstanding these
Thracians' degradation and notorious barbarousness, both
as to language and manners, still to these prehistoric
Thracians belong the Muses and the cultivation of
music, Orpheus, Musaeus Thamyris and Eumolpus;
thus proving that it does not necessarily follow that
the man enslaved is inferior intellectually to the en-
slaver. It is impossible, however, in a talk so limited
to treat, as elaborately as desired, Grecian slavery. It
was said by Demosthenes that the slave in Athens was
better off than the free citizen of many other countries.

ROMAN SLAVERY

differed in many particulars from that of Greece. All
men, by natural law in Rome, were free; and to be anything else was contrary to that law. However, by the
law of nations, a captive, instead of being slain, was called
servus quasi servatus. Also a free man had power to
sell himself. The early history of the Romans tells us
that the owner had the power of punishing and even put-
ting to death his slave. Whenever Vedius Pollio got
mad he dashed such slaves as displeased him into his
fish ponds to feed his lampreys, and when the polite
Augustus, the emperor, was told about this slave-holder's
conduct, the severest punishment the emperor inflicted
upon him was the destruction of the pond. Under
Claudius extreme cruel treatment of slaves was forbidden, and in selling them parents could not be separated

from children; the same was true concerning brothers and sisters. The children of a female slave followed the status of the mother. A slave could not contract marriage, and no legal relation was recognized between parent and child. The harboring of a runaway slave was illegal. Persons in good circumstances kept an immense number, one person often owning two hundred, to have a large number being a matter of ostentation. Originally, as here, the slave was allowed to own nothing, he and all he acquired being his master's. But when a slave commenced to work in the "trades," as in this country, a certain part of his gains was given him as his own, which he might keep until it amounted to sufficient to purchase his freedom. Justinian and Christianity did much towards the overthrow and extinction of slavery, but failed to accomplish it, and slavery continued even after the fall of the empire.

During the middle ages this "curse" merged into a mitigated condition called serfdom, which prevailed all over Europe, the taint of which has not even yet been entirely wiped out. Though early modern times stopped the selling of slaves in Europe, the Mohammedan nations would, as often as they captured a Christian of Europe, sell him into Asia or Africa. Many of the brightest minds of Europe can trace their ancestry back to the home of the serf. Instead of being ashamed of his low condition, he is thankful that he is not despised because of a God-fixed position, but honored because he is found to possess innate qualities powerful enough to lift him up out of the black night of serfdom into the broad daylight of citizenship.

The slaves of the Romans were not Negroes. The term of *slave* is taken from the word *slavonic,* the Slavonians, many of them being made bondsmen, were called by the name *slave.*

NEGRO SLAVERY

followed as a sequel to the discovery of America. The Negroes of Africa, like other savage races, enslaved those captives that they did not put to death. Along the coast of Guinea the Arabs engaged extensively in the slave business. The Aborigines proving too weak for plantation and mine work, the Portugese, who possessed and controlled a large part of the coast of Africa,

began the work of selling Africans. The other coloni-
zers of the new world soon followed. Hayti was
the first place to which Africans were carried. Bishop
LasCassas, on account of the fatality of labor to the constitution of the Aboriginal population, obtained the
consent of Charles to substitute Negro for Indian labor.
In 1517, the Portugese brought from the coast of Guinea
to St. Domingo, Hayti, a cargo of vanquished Africans,
who, from that time, were slaves.

Then comes Sir John Hawkins, the first Englishman
to soil his hands in the traffic, in which his countrymen
soon largely participated. Between the years 1680 and
1700, England exported from Africa more than 300,000
Africans to be used as slaves. From 1700 to 1786 England carried into Jamaica alone 610,000 slaves. The
greatest inhumanity was used in shipping them, the ves-
sels being so overcrowded that a large number would die
in the passage. So cruel was slavery in the British colonies of America, that England had to throw legal re-
straints around the owners, controlling largely their conduct toward their slaves Courts were established to hear
the slaves' complaints; their condition was to a certain extent changed for the better, and the whipping of women
was forbidden. Notwithstanding slavery was permitted
and legally sanctioned in the British colonies, it was the
law in England that, when a slave put his foot on English
soil, he became free, provided he remained on English
soil; if he returned to the colonies his owner could re-
claim him. Why this law was made is not stated. Very
few owners, it is needless to say, were willing to have
their slaves visit England with them. Thirteen years
after the settlement of Jamestown, Virginia, a Dutch
vessel landed in said harbor with twenty or more Afri-
can slaves. In 1776, there had been about 300,000 Africans imported into the British Colonies, from the time
of their first settlement. The first census recorded
697,897; this was in 1790, every State in the Union being
represented except Massachusetts, which at this time included Maine. This State had abolished slavery in 1780.
It is often erroneously believed by many that the State
made immortal by the blood of the brave Negro, Crispus
Attucks, was the State to first set the black man free.
The first State to take the step was Vermont, in 1777.

New York, Rhode Island, Connecticut, New Jersey and Pennsylvania commenced the work of gradual emancipation, New York abolishing it in 1827; the two smallest States having only a few slaves left in 1840; Pennsylvania having at that time only sixty-four to be freed, and New Jersey in 1850 with 236 still in bondage. Washington, Jefferson, Franklin, Hamilton and a number of other leaders of public opinion were opposed to slavery on moral and religious grounds: *and not less a' a system calculated to become a retarding influence as to he progress of civilization and the general advancement of the people.* In spite of the adverse opinion of these statesmen, in 1820, the slaves numbered 1,538,022, in 1830, 2,009.043, in 1840, 2,487,455, in 1850, 3,204,313; in 1860, 3,953,760 The organization for its abolishment, which was formed in Pennsylvania in 1775 had never ceased to work. Eli Whitney, of Massachusetts, who invented the cotton gin in 1793, is largely responsible for the increase in slaves and the general interest manifested in the traffic. It is said that Massachusetts, Vermont and the other New England States were freed of slaves on account of their climate being too cold and their lands for farming purposes too sterile to make the slaves of any profit It is also said that the slave owners in the States referred to sold their slaves South, and took the money derived from said sale and invested it in lands, improving of their section and in manufacturing industries. It is also stated that when they noticed the profit accruing from the slave business to the Southern owner, by reason of the congeniality of the climate, the cry went up that, "Free labor has in slave labor an unfair competitor "

During the time the system continued in the South, while there were many who abused their power in every way, there were those among the slave-holders who were filled with kindness always for those they owned. Slavery prepared the Negro in every way for citizenship except one: it did not teach him responsibility. American slavery, if nothing more to the Negro, must always be considered at least an opportunity Slavery, in this country, taught the Negro obedience: and he who would be obeyed must himself first learn to obey Slavery taught him industry, sobriety and economy. To have him learn all this was to his owner's advantage. Another phase of

the slavery question presents itself   As the Negro represented property, the owner was careful to provide for him,
in most instances, proper food, clothing and medical attention.   To strike certain Negroes would endanger the safety
of your life, white man though you might be   The slave's
master would protect him against attacks from the white
race.   Many a fight has taken place between white men of
the South in defence of the Negro   The Negro could
do anything; however flagrant a violation of the law it
might be a sound " flogging " was the extent of the
punishment (with only few exceptions).   As a slave, he
was often promoted to a position of first rank among
slaves, his duty being to " eavesdrop " and " Negro-drive "
The white children were raised up on the most familiar
terms with the black children, the only difference being
that from the time the little colored child could talk it was
instructed to regard the young white child as " young
master " or " young missis," and that its first duty was to
render complete obedience   Often this " young master "
or " young missis " would be found slipping "dainties "
from the table for his or her favorite " darkey "   This relation was increased, and an affinity between the two races,
which is still present, was the result.   The old colored
woman was seen often, with the children around her, telling about " brer fox," " brer rabbit" and the "Jack-o-
lantern."

The old colored man can be seen making blow guns,
bird traps and telling ghost stories, all to amuse these
young white children.   Witness the nursing of these
white children by " black mammies " and " black dad-
dies," and you can readily understand why they genu-
inely love each other.   Listen at the plaintive ditties, and
at times light-hearted melodies, and you will find even
the hair on your head in sympathy with their natural
" airs."   While all this is taking place, and life to all ap-
pearances to both seems worth living, "free labor" and
"slave labor" engage each other in debate; the argument
becomes heated; they clutch each the other, and lookers-
on can see that it is a fight to the death   After four years
of the hardest and most cruel fighting known to mankind, "free labor" whips and declares that, " neither slavery nor involuntary servitude, except as a punishment
for crime, whereof the party shall have been duly con-

victed, shall exist within the United States, or any place subject to their jurisdiction. Congress shall have power to enforce this article by appropriate legislation " Then came the change. "Young master" and "young missis" of the day before could see from the general stir and excitement that something extraordinary had taken place Those humble and obedient young negroes had all at once become entirely metamorphosed When called they did not answer as respectfully as theretofore nor did they move as quickly The only ones who appeared the same, although looking exceedingly well pleased and happy about something, were the old people, "daddy" and "mammy " God bless them! they were in a quandary; they hardly knew what to do. "Massa Linkum done gone and sot us free, and now we must go and leave de ole plantation. What's gwine become of ole massa and ole missis ?" A few, here and there, are still on the old plantation trying to determine what they shall do. Poor creatures, they will die there, and their graves will be somewhere on that old plantation and among those who shed a real, earnest tear will be found a white face. It is this kind of pure love which I confidently believe will keep the "ship of State," on which rides both races, safe, until the harbor is reached, the vessel is anchored, the life boat is lowered and all are safely landed.

CHAPTER II

THE WHITE MAN AND THE NEGRO AS EMPLOYER AND EMPLOYE

The once slave is now a free man No one is responsible for his well-being but himself His house, his raiment and his food he must earn in winter and in summer The once humble slave drinks in the atmosphere of freedom and holds up his head. Loves a "Yankee" or Northern man as he loves his Saviour. Learns to hate the former owner that once he loved to obey The former master sees in this changed condition the Negro becoming intolerant—an eyesore and a thorn in the flesh. Unlike heretofore, the Negro stops before going to work to know what pay he is going to receive as remunera-

tion for his labor. The subject of contract is discussed
on equal terms, the Negro often refusing to work because the amount offered is not commensurate with his
idea of the service to be performed. The man who once
owned so many Negroes, that he really did not know all
of their names, must now be humiliated by inviting the
laborer to discuss with him the justice of the "wage"
offered The man once rich as slave owner, now poor
from the results of war, sees the Negroes he once
owned, many of them, living surrounded by as many
comforts as he Can you be guilty of surprise, if an unpleasant word is uttered by him, who was once in the
"lap of luxury," now so degraded by freedom? The
sensible man fully appreciates the feeling which comes
over a man once rich, when he observes the individual
he once owned with a "silk hat" on his head, standing
collar around his neck, a ruffled bosom shirt adorning
his front, and a long-tailed coat covering his back, set
off by 'English bottom" pants, fitting neatly over his
patent leather shoes, while he, who once owned the
now full blown dandy, is in want. He speaks to this
black Chesterfieldian, and, as his reward, is impudently
scowled at for having done so—the two men, representatives of different races, honestly mistaken concerning
the true condition of the mind of each towards the other.
The unscrupulous politician has done his poisonous and
deadly work. The colored man regards this old man
who once owned him as one of the greatest sinners in
the world. To think that he should have been held in
bondage so long is to so insult his *new feeling* as a free
man, that he pledges himself never to forgive the sin
committed against him as long as he lives He takes
no time to think about the great work of civilization,
which has been performed on his behalf. He takes no
time to remember that if he had been white, living So th,
he would have done the same thing. He forgets entirely that there were plenty of men who held slaves,
not because they loved the system, loved to enslave their
fellows, but because it was legal and because it was believed by them to be a source for increasing their revenue. A great many Southern men found themselves,
by the custom of the country, forced to maintain the "institution," many of them having all of their wealth

wrapped up in "blacks" left to them by their parents, or purchased from the men of the North, who found no profit in the "blacks" The colored man, when thinking about the "old" *regime*, "the before the war times," is so filled with prejudice that he is unable to give an honest, fair, unbiased opinion

There are men to-day engaged in selling alcoholic drinks to their neighbors, carrying on what is known as the saloon business, not because they love that kind of work (they despise it), but because it is legal many others are following it, because it pays larger profits than any other occupation they can find. It is not right to hate a man for engaging in a "traffic" when he found that calling the rule in the community where he lived with not even an exception, among those who were able to buy slaves. Bishops, preachers, doctors, lawyers, merchants, farmers, everybody who wanted to be respectable, had to have a factotum, a Negro. Men gave their daughters and sons when marrying a slave, as a beginning in their new life. When this picture is honestly looked at, the Negro will find he is unable to hate the white man who owned slaves, and the white man will not confess himself guilty of gross wrong-doing for having so owned them for a time, except where those held were abused. It is not believed that it was the plan of God that slavery should always exist. It may be that God intended that the poor Indians, beaten back and destroyed, until hardly one of them is left to tell the story, should have in the Negro an afflicting nemesis, who, through slavery's "cruel season," should learn the "walks" of civilized man, and out of these civilized Negroes should come the civilizing and christianizing of the whole world. It may be that the "penance" exacted for the harsh and cruel treatment of the Indians was the civilizing and bringing to the truth the inhabitants of Africa. "That which you measure out to men shall be meted out to you again" It is stated that the two races of the South, holding the relation of employer and laborer, are honestly mistaken about each other. This is true. The picture of the Negro regarding the white man as a great sinner for having held him has been exhibited. The Negro believes that the white man of the South is eternally and everlastingly opposed to his elevation, this lesson having been taught him by the

unscrupulous politicians, of carpet-bag times, who swarm-
ed over this section like the flies did in Egypt upon a certain historic occasion The Negro being emancipated,
empty handed, without anything, not so much as a place
to lay his head, fell an easy prey to the human, graveyard hyenas, "whose insides crave continually to live on
the blood of this recently made free individual." Then it
was that the Southern white man made mistake number
two. Instead of closing in around these blacks, and giving them to understand that although they were free the
Southern white man was their friend, you either stood still
and refused to do anything, or said· "Let them go.
They are free. Let the d——d yankees have them, or
let them starve to death " A great many pious, Christian hearted property owners of the South did proceed
to make terms with these liberated people; but even these,
for a number of years after the war, treated the Negro
with indifference. Hence, the Negro was found drifting
farther and farther away from the white people of the
South—a people dear to him in every particular. Many
outrages were committed upon these blacks by that class
of poor whites who formed a scab on every community
before the war, and who never received from the slave
owners the recognition and warm treatment they meted
out to the slaves. This poor, miserable class of whites
thought that to afflict the manumitted black man was
to gain for them the approval and applause of the rich
people, or the ' bone and sinew" of this section. Although the proclamation of Mr. Lincoln was declared in
operation from the first day of January, 1863, it was fully
two years later before the colored man in *these parts* was
given to understand that he was his "own boss." Many
of the colored people made this mistake: They defined
"freedom" to mean that they were masters of their own
time; and "liberty" to mean that they had no use for it,
and they practiced the definition to the strictness of the
letter Another mistake was a failure to distinguish
between *humility* and *politeness*. Very few colored men
who wanted to stand well in colored circles, or in their
own opinions, as free men, would suffer themselves to
pull off their hats when entering the homes and par-
lors of those who formerly owned them. Such a complete change in conduct added its help towards driving

away from the minds of the whites any "compromise
policy" benefiting the Negro   The cry went up that
the Negroes, once oppressed, were becoming oppressors.
The blacks, many of them, expected a division of the
lands and other property to be made, and the *strange
political parasites*, who pretended to represent the Moses
family, come to lead the "blacks" from the Egypt of op-
pression to the Canaan of idleness and plenty, were very
careful to keep them thinking so   All this added fuel to
the fire, filling the blacks with hate for their *own white
folks*, and their *own* - *hite folks* with anger towards them
for being so easily imposed upon.   Often was the "forty
acres and a mule" discussed: often were they told they
should get them; often did they look in vain, to see the
promise fulfilled   And so it was   Instead of the races
here coming to an amicable settlement of a "future
policy" to be pursued by both, without outside
interference, they were set aside by the worn-out
politicians of another section, who could see in the
South's new condition a rich field of grain to harvest,
the poor Negro as usual coming in for the "blows
and cuffs" given by the whites, whose indignation had
gone beyond control   Poor men of a dark hue, truly
you have been more sinned against than sinning   During
all the long years of war, when every able bodied white
man had left home for the "front of battle" or to do work
in the Confederate halls of legislation, you, with that faith-
fulness which distinguished you as among the noblest
sons of God, remained at "old master's" home and pro-
tected, fed and clothed his family   You never allowed
them to suffer or want for anything which the farm or
the woods could produce.   When "old master" and
"young master" returned from war, you, at first glimpse,
were as glad to see them as were their families tied to
them by the ties of consanguinity, and when you ran up
to bid them welcome you were bidden, in a great majority of cases, to "be off with you to your yankee
friends"   For three years your life as a "free laborer"
has been filled with thorns.   Men have been allowed to
vent their spite on you, for their defeat in war   Chain-
gangs and penitentiaries have been and are being replen-
ished from among your ranks.   The woman, who, on
leaving *the place of her service*, takes a "few scraps"

or "morsels of food" to feed her "young" at home, is stopped, searched, the provision found (sent to jail), comes to trial, is convicted and sentenced to probably six months at hard labor in the chaingang The children at home, with hungry stomachs and weeping eyes, that night (filled with grief) sleep in an old deserted and cheerless house, alone. No tidings of "mammy" has reached them. Next day, the next, and for weeks, no "mammy" comes Poor little children, "mammy" is working at hard labor in the chaingang for trying to make her way home with "refused morsels," which she little dreamed, at the time she took them, would be called stealing. The little children—one takes sick, dies and is buried; cause, want of food and proper attention. Another, ten years old, is so hungry that he seizes an apple or a dozen peanuts; he thinks no one sees him; he is so ravenously hungry that all he sees is something to eat Poor little fellow, you were discovered and ere you have had time to eat the apple, or the peanuts, a policeman has hand cuffed you, and your doom is fixed. The apple or peanuts are given back to the confectioner or fruit dealer and you are marched to the "lock up." still hungry. Why didn't you ask for the apple? says one "Because sir. I knew I would be refused, and I was so hungry I could not resist the temptation." Why don't you work? "Mammy is paid such small wages that she cannot afford me decent clothes, and no one will hire me to work for them in the plight I am in " The judge, next morning in the court room, states that it is his duty to stop petty thieving. He inquires for the boy's mother, and is told she is not in the court room He then says to the little fellow, "I will fine you $50 00 and cost, or six months " The judge would have been just as humane if he had said one million dollars and cost, or six months It means the same to the boy,—six months in the chaingang In one sense it is a kind act, for he will now get a glimpse of his "mammy" who is also there. The sad sight will be to see the "mammy," whose time will be out sooner than her tender child's, taking her leave of him Oh, God! Thou who hearest the widows and the orphans when they pray, surely Thou canst hear the groans of such creatures as these. Yes, for Thou art no respecter of persons Oh, you Christian hearted people, you, who give large sums to build fine churches and to carry the gospel into heathen lands, can you not make happy and comfortable the condition and home of your ebony-hued neighbor who felled your forests, built up your cities, made you rich and remained as an impregnable adamantine wall around your family during those long years of misery and bloodshed? Suppose the blacks, as freedmen, do try, many of them, to act independently and dress with neatness: they are copying after you, and you ought to encourage them in imitating the virtues of your race to the entire exclusion of the vices. They are used to your ways, they are acclimated, they are frugal and they are earnest workers. You therefore ought not to suffer any little, puny, superficial prejudice, based on a false sentiment, to drive you apart, as employer and employé. But before you have time to agree to pay him fair wages for his hire, to allow him a chance to buy land, build neat homes, raise up a virtuous family, do business for himself, affording him equal opportunities to live and be happy, and thereby running out the "carpet bag" element, a message comes from Washington, that the slave, made free by the thirteenth article of amendment, ratified in 1865, has another to go with it, the fourteenth amendment, constituted of five sections. The first declaring all persons born or naturalized in the United States to be citizens, and prohibiting the States from passing laws which do not bear equally upon all: that is, forbidding class legislation. The second section apportioning representation among the States according to their numbers, based on all the people of their respective States except untaxed Indians, and declaring that when any number of male citizens, being twenty-one years of age, were denied the right to vote in national or State elections, except for participation in rebellion or other crime, then the representation was to be proportionately reduced. This section was to take away the representation of the South allowed, for the Negroes as slaves, in Congress, unless said freedmen were allowed to vote. The third section disqualifies any man who, having ever taken an oath as State or national officer, or to support the Constitution of the United States, afterwards engaging in insurrection and rebellion against the Union, from holding any national office whatever; and it was also provided that Con-

gress, by a two-third vote, could remove said disabilities.
The fourth section made valid the public debt, declaring
that debts made in suppressing rebellions shall never be
questioned, and also providing that no countenance should
ever be given by the government to debts incurred in
aid of insurrection and rebellion against the United States
or for the loss or emancipation of slaves, all such debts
and obligations being held illegal and void. The fifth
and last provides that Congress is empowered to enforce
this amendment by legislation, which amendment was rat-
ified in 1868 This enactment of course made the Negro
more strong, for it not only made him a full-fledged citizen, with a citizenship which knew no legal inequality, but
it also practically made him a voter, as it made him a
witness, a juror and a man capable of holding office under
the government of the United States. Like all "new
departures," this innovation found in the people, "landed,"
of the South opposition This is what may be called
Democratic mistake number three It is firmly believed
that had the Democrats welcomed this law and followed
it up by asking for the fifteenth amendment to the National Constitution, expressing   "The right of citizens of
the United States to vote shall not be denied or abridged
by the United States or by any State on account of race,
color or previous condition of servitude;" that the colored
slave, who had *merged* into freedman, into citizen and into
voter, would have naturally by reason of long acquaintance
with the white man of this section, clasped hands
with the Democrats and prevented the ignorant, extrava
gant, outrageous, heartrending and sickening scenes which
were presented during the reconstruction period. But the
Anglo-Saxon of the South refused to shake hands with the
free, enfranchised Ethiopian. The abuse which should,
if showered at all, have been poured upon the heads of
the white men, carpet-baggers, was instead made to
deluge the Negro. In the book called "An appeal to
Pharaoh" it is stated· "*The Negro was the cause of the
division of the United States into the two sections, the
North and the South, and has been the cause of all the
strife that has taken place between those sections since
the independence of the colonies was established.*" Without stopping to prove how false is this quoted statement, it is true, that the Negro, whenever it is possi-

ble to make him such, is always made a "scape-goat, for
every wrong committed. But during this "reconstruction period," the Negro, though misunderstood, was found,
in spite of cares, sorrows, troubles and afflictions, more
happy than his white neighbor, spending his dollar with
a reckless disregard for the future, that would put a
millionaire to shame, light hearted, sunshiny and full
of joy even at a funeral, camp meeting or a hanging
here and there, buying a little piece of land, building a
neat cottage and exampling after the other race in bringing up a respectable family, working hard all day, frolick-
ing all night or nearly so, but fresh and ready for work
next morning. This is the life he was leading when the
ballot was placed in his hand. Freedom obtained as a
war measure, suffrage given as a political exigency. The
former prayed for, but hardly expected, the latter found
him not only unprepared but surprised. The once nonen-
tity now an entity, equal in every way to the highest
in the land from a *before the law* standpoint, with
power to make or unmake congressmen, governors and
presidents. Had this increased "mark" of the government's consideration been given as a merited and de-
served gift or without the hope of reward, it would have
made the donors archangels of the first brightness in that
city of eternal light. It was not, however, so given. In
fact the Negro can truthfully say that all he has received
has been given him out of necessity. He was freed
that the Southern army might be crippled and conquered.
He was enfranchised that the union people and Republican party might remain in power. The politicians who
favored giving the Negro the ballot predicted and
prophesied how he would vote when given the power.
Let us see if their prophecies came true. Why did not
the South free the blacks? Why did not the owners of
the South make free men and women out of those who
had made their crops and enriched them, and had nursed
their children into manhood and womanhood? Why did
the Southern owners wait for strangers to come and do
this noble act? Why did you not do these things and
go down in history to be forever known as race
redeemers? It is not yet too late to cover yourselves all
over with honor and glory. Refuse to stay back in the
dead past, but make fleet your feet and rush on, still

more rapidly on, with this, the age of progress, to the golden goal which, if you will, awaits you.

<hr>

CHAPTER III

THE WHITE MAN AND THE NEGRO AS CITIZENS AND CITIZEN

All male persons, except untaxed Indians, without regard to color, that cared to do so, of legal age and not under any disability by reason of having committed crime of some sort, voted in 1872   It is said that a thorough canvass was made of the colored voters and they were told that thenceforth their creed should read I believe in God the Father Almighty maker of Heaven and earth, and in the Republican party equal to his only begotten son, which party was conceived by Garrison, Phillips, Thad. Stevens and Sumner   and born of Abraham Lincoln   His trinity to worship, was God the Father, Christ the Son, and the Republican party, three in one   And never was smoke more inclined to ascend upward, water to seek its level and the world to rotate upon its axis, than were the colored people disposed to vote the Republican ticket. You could give the black man employment as you did. send your doctor to see him and his family when sick. lend him money when in trouble, clothe him when naked   feed him when hungry: build his churches for him   establish schools for the intellectual training of his children. bury those of his family who died   tell him that you were willing, if you outlived him to see that he was decently interred: still, on election day, he would go up to the polls and vote against you   Perhaps you might on perfect equality, sit down and commence to talk with him about his political enmity and ballot antagonism towards you and your interest   His reply would be, to all you said   "I like you; I appreciate your kindness to me and my family, but you are a Democrat.   Mr. B , who is running against you for the office, I do not like him personally as well as I like you, but he is a Republican, and I must vote for him " You state to him that, if he votes against you and thereby causes the other man's election, he will make you poorer and less able to help him when he wants aid. The statement comes forth from him "I must vote the Republican ticket let what will come " You tell him that the man who is running against you for the office is a stranger in the community that he owns very little if anything at all, and that you two ought to agree to stand together because your interests are identical, what benefiting the one benefiting the other He is still unmoved and says, "you are a Democrat—if all the Democrats were like you it would be another thing (not that he would vote for you), but they are not and I must stand to my party " Election day came, and there they were, one right behind the other, like a lot of sheep, all voting the same ticket, believing to do otherwise would be to sin against the Holy Ghost You cannot blame them You refused, when returning home from the war, to extend the olive branch of political peace and make friends of them, and in that way possessing yourself of their strength, which would have been a powerful lever for your weal The despicable political tramps, who saw, in your cold and indifferent treatment of the Negro, their bonanza, hurried to his cabin, whispered in his ear, "all white men are not alike, we love you, give us the offices and we will protect you. Fall down and worship us and all we have shall be given you." How faithfully the black voters worshipped is well remembered. Who can forget their Moses of South Carolina and their Chamberlain Talk about the Negro s fidelity No people on earth are more faithful, when once you gain their confidence, than the black I have known a Jacob to cheat his Esau. I have known a Judas to betray his Lord I have known an Arnold to forsake h s country, but I have never known a sensible Negro to desert his admitted friend It would have been surprising if the colored race had voted any ticket save the ticket of Lincoln, John Brown and Grant. Out on a tempestuous sea, with a leaking barque and an inexperienced crew, what was more natural than for them, gladly, to allow themselves to make for the harbor which appeared the most inviting They voted in the white polit-

ical scums they thought to be their dearest friends, but
who, in fact, proved themselves their greatest enemies
The right to vote for carries with it the right to be voted
for   The colored voter became anxious for office and the
cry of "it's not time" was powerless to hold them back.
Then it was that these wily, cunning, political white
tricksters got together and said 'boys our *political drift
wood*, our *hobby horses*, our *stuffed clubs* to whale the
political life out of Democrats are *waking up*, they are
growing discontented and restless, listen how they howl
for *gore*, *spoils* and *pie* of office.   We must give them
recognition, and this is what we will do·   We will select
the least competent from among them and to these we
will add a few sharp unscrupulous ones   Their conduct
in office will be such as to justly cause wide-spread
complaint, and then we will say, now, black boys, you see
we told you the truth   "*It's not time.*"   The result was
a number of justices of the peace were elected who could
not read their names   Men of color were sent to the
legislature of the State as representatives and senators that
actually could not tell the time of day, and as for being
able to write intelligently very few could answer guilty
to the charge.   This statement is not made to the dis-
credit of these unfortunate blacks, who literally, like Cin-
cinnatus of old, were called from their ploughs to take
upon themselves the · official ermine" as judges and law-
makers for the people, they did the best they knew how,
many of them   It is to the shame of the radical Republican dictators, that these truthful statements are made   A
colored man, who by hard study and work was, in every
particular, fit to represent the people, would never be selected by them   He would want to stop and read
"measures" presented before voting for them; sometime
he would disagree with the leaders, and balk their plans,
hence it was a part of their duty to see to it, that the intelligent, representative Negroes were kept out of office.
They usually hunted around for some voluble, ignorant
black man, who called himself a preacher, and who en-
tertained his audience by sound and tone, appealing to
their passion rather than to their reason.

Such a black man, who, while preaching, would carry
his hand up to his ears and encourage plaintive groaning
and melancholy moaning, they would make their leader

They found him easily flattered; calling him the "smartest Negro" in his county or settlement filled him with unspeakable joy. The Negro who voted the Democratic ticket, if it was found out, had to be very careful not to be caught out of reach of a white man, for, if he was, the other Negroes discharged what they felt to be a religious duty, and that was, to give him a severe "thrashing." His mother and father disowned him for such an act, his wife left him, if he was married, if single, his lover refused to receive him, the little black children yelled at him, calling him old "demercrat nigger;" his church turned him out; his preacher consigned him to a lake which burneth with brimstone and fire forever and forever; and more sad than all the rest, though honest he might be, a considerable number of Democrats seemed eager to tell him that they had no confidence in him. Daniel in the den of lions was in Heaven compared with the place where rested the pioneer Negro Democrat. It is stated that mothers of the Negro race changed the little prayer repeated by their children to read

> Now I lay me down to sleep,
> I want to be a Republican
> If I should die before I wake,
> I want to be a Republican
> I pray the Lord my soul to take,
> If I have been a Republican
> All of which I ask for Jesus' sake,
> Because I am a Republican

In England every public entertainment, of every character, high or low, indicates the close or conclusion by singing, 'God save the Queen.' I think the English could learn a lesson from these parents with black faces Regardless of this loyalty, the Republican party has been as false to the Negro voters as sheol would be to a powder house within its confines. For more than seventeen years of unswerving devotion and uncompromising loyalty they have paid the Negro rebuffs, insults, inattention, broken pledges and promises, until to-day he stands uncovered before the world as the most abject, cowardly cringing, political slave that the world has ever seen His schools on every hill, his colleges in every State, one million and a half boys and girls in the school-room, preachers and teachers by the thousands, professional men by the hundreds, mechanics and tradesmen by the car loads, and farmers without number, millions of dollars worth of property, newspapers and inventions, but with all these, still a race of political cowards, *quasi* foreigners, and, so far as suffrage is concerned, perfect nondescripts or nobodies. College professors of the race, our prize orators in black, Douglas, Bruce, Langston Lynch Smalls, Turner, Scarborough, Pinchback, Smyth, Barnett, Townsend, Gibbs, Straker, Purvis, Cook, Simmons, Crummell, Downing, Page, Price, Crogman, Lee, Mitchell, Arnett, Wilson, Williams, Patty and the hundreds of other distinguished Negroes in this country, all together, don't amount to anything in the councils of the Republican party. They are used as so many puppets in a side show, set up as targets to be riddled, humiliated, disgraced and destroyed. You must wear the Republican yoke without murmur, or the uncle-zips of the Negro race, will politically kill you, because bidden to do so by the party bosses.

"He who would be free must himself first strike the blow." Ten or a dozen white men, staunch, true and tried Republicans are all you can find in any one of the Southern States. I mean white Republicans who will support a Negro, if he is nominated in a Republican convention. I doubt whether the Southern States will average over six white men, in each of them, answering to the description just stated. Notwithstanding, the Republican party in each State of the South with not more than one white man to every thousand Negroes in it, is dictated and controlled entirely by the white members. The white Republican boss in Georgia, representing 143,471 black voters by the census of 1880, and about twenty-five white Republicans, himself included to make the number, absolutely controls the whole affair for his party, without having so much as a colored advisory board. And the colored citizen filled with cowardice submits, with one white Republican to every 6,000 Negro voters in Georgia, all of whom are professedly, Republicans; the patronage (from Washington under an administration put in by Negro solidity in voting) is given to white men. Whenever a Negro begins to make a noise, he is sent for, and if he is somewhat influential he is given an appointment to last until they can rob him of his influence. The appointment is generally given to him out of his district. After they have "killed" him with his people, he is put under the political ax and that is the last we hear of him, except as a warning to other ambitious men of the race. This *destroyer of the Negro race* and the poor man (the Republican party) has established manufactories throughout the South One of the chief lessons they attempt to have the student to learn is his entire dependence upon their institutions, and that he must let his instructors do his thinking in every particular. How long, how long, will the colored race remain in the chains of the "monster?" Why do not the men I have named cry out? Resign your "spittoon position," go work and sweat for a living, but what you cry out against the iniquities of the Republican party which is now nothing more, so far as principle is concerned, than a "putrid reminiscence" Like Mahone, is the Republican party The negro is all right until he wants to go to Congress or hold office, and then he is only fit to be put to death

How long will the colored race cast more than twice as many votes as were cast in the State of New York, without getting as many appointments as there are in little Rhode Island. Office is not all. But a party which lives on "the dead past" for pelf, spoil and office, ought to be made to give some sort of tangible recognition to those who make it possible for that party to have a president to *dish* out the offices. All the troubles between the races originate out of politics, to the detriment and injury of the Negro, who gets no political *bread and butter* for his pay Destroy the bakery and the baker unless there is an immediate change. Try another political cook When you prove to the people of the South that you understand individual responsibility as a citizen: when you show the owners of this section that you no longer wait for a certain part of their race to come and tie them and deliver them over to you, when you show them that you are willing to appreciate favors conferred that you are making friends wherever you can, and that you are no longer filled with prejudice towards them, then will come your political emancipation, and with it all that any other citizen enjoys in keeping with your intelligence, wealth and numbers Social equality the sensible Negro despises, civil liberty and justice is what he desires.

The one is based on natural selection and choice: the other upon equity and good conscience.

CHAPTER IV.

THE PROBLEM—MUST THERE BE A RACE CONFLICT?

Many strange and peculiar things are taking place in our country. Certainly within the last six or eight months there has been more complaint about the unsettled condition of affairs between the races, than at any time preceding the period mentioned and the inauguration of Rutherford B. Hayes. During the campaign of 1874, the colored people were told by Republican "stump" speakers, that Democratic ascendency, Democratic victory, would be followed by all of the colored people being put back into slavery. That with the election of a Democratic president would come the paying off of the debt incurred in raising the insurrection and rebellion against the government, that the slaves would be paid for, with interest ; and that the Confederate soldiers would be pensioned. A Democratic president was, however, elected Although the intelligent Negroes of the country did not believe that there was a possibility of their re-enslavement, there were millions of poor " ignorants" who did fear that such would be the result, and when " these" heard of Cleveland's induction into office great was their alarm Public meetings had to be held in a number of places to reassure them of their perfect freedom under a Democratic administration as well as under a Republican. One old colored man, before the report reached him that all was safe, had cut his throat and entered the great beyond In another case, the facts showed an old man, with his personal property, making his way back to his old master's home, saying, when questioned about it: "I am not gwine to wait for 'em to come after me, I am gwine back myself." After much talk it was fully explained to him how the administration could change hands politically without interfering with his rights, liberties and privileges as a free man, in the least. He returned home rebuking himself for being so foolish as to have considered seriously the possibility o his again being made a slave. Mr. Cleveland entered the presidential office and left no stone unturned, which had for its trend and intendment the proving to the Negro, beyond question, that his rights were just as secure under Democratic as under Republican rule He did all he could to teach the black race, that all men, without regard to color or previous condition, were equal before the law Political figures showed that very few Negroes voted for Cleveland In spite of their opposition and solidly voting against him and his party, Mr Cleveland did not hold them answerable, but like the noble man that he was, and is to-day, freely forgave them their political trespasses, and proceeded to deal out offices to them with a lavish hand One of the best paying offices in the government, he gave to a black man, Lawyer J. C Matthews, of Albany, New York, and after his rejection by a Republican senate, on the grounds of his being a non-resident, Mr. Cleveland sent him back by reappointment to the senate, and again they rejected him, ostensibly because he was a non-resident of the District of Columbia but really because he was a Negro who dared to do his own thinking, bidding defiance from the campaign of 1872, to the Republican party lash and party whip Still this Democratic president, who is the grandest living humanitarian, sent to the senate another Negro, James Monroe Trotter, who was also a non resident, and one who alleged that he was his own "political boss" The senate of the United States "chewed crow" and confirmed him, knowing, as they did, that Mr Cleveland would order a carload of Negroes to Washington but what that office should go to the Negro race Office after office was given to the Negroes by him recommendations in reference to the ' Freedman's Bank' and the ' Republic of Liberia" were sent to the senate Hence, when the Republicans decided, preceding the assembling of their convention, that the antipathy of Democrats towards Negroes would not be as powerful a weapon as it had been they were puzzled to know what to do in order to stir the voters up The message of Mr Cleveland, asking for a reduction of the tariff, was declared to be their shibboleth Their old man of the sea (Blaine), who was away in Italy, hastened to cablegram the under men of the Republican host what position to take. " We will forget the Negro and say protection *versus* free tiade." They went to the "countiy' with that cry, and through misrepresentations, the use of money and superior party management, they won, and Harrison was declared elected. All at once, the Negro, who in the campaign was forgotten, again came into prominence as a vexatious subject Newspaper after newspaper was filled with column after column of news about the Negro Everywhere you go one hears nothing discussed but the race question, men who want to be known as statesmen declaring that they see trouble coming to the country on account of the presence of two distinct races living here together—races that have lived together 250 years

Mrs Canfield is so moved that she must write a private letter, for the public, in which she sees the storm, and prays for some secure place in the skies, where she can look down and see "black heels on white necks." General Sherman catches the disease, and tells the colored men to "start the trouble and the North will help" Albion W. Tourgee is very sick, and speaks of the power in conflict; and so with Cable and a number of others. The discussion of the subject intensifies the feeling here and makes sober men drunk, all scared, frightened, shaking with race ague, when really what so claims their attention in the day and keeps them awake at night, after all, is only a shadow on the wall, a bubble on the wave, a political spook originated by politicians on one side to hold the Negro back, and discussed on the other to keep the South solid for the South's protection: protection not so much against the Negro, as against those white persons who use the Negro for their own selfish good. There are a number of Republicans who are anxious to have the Negro see something serious in the race question, for they, as the Negro's pretended best friends, will have to settle the question or solve the problem; and while this is being done, of course the Negro must continue to do whatever they tell him. In a talk about the matter with a *Columbus Enquirer-Sun* reporter I said, in answer to his remark,

"What do you think of the race question?"

"It is being made serious by the attention given to it. It is exceedingly strange to me that there should be so much anxiety and interest on either side. The Negroes and white people lived here together nearly two hundred and fifty years prior to emancipation friendly and without clashing, and I don't see why they cannot continue to do so for a million years, notwithstanding the relation of master and slave has been changed to employer and employé. The talk of getting rid of the Negro to make room for the foreigners, who come from the old country and refuse to come South, instead of Northwest, on account of their dislike of Negro competition and association is utter foolishness. No laborer can be found in the world able to take the place of the colored man in this section. You may not raise cotton, and still the Negro will be needed. The white laborers will force from you, when they come here, should you try the experiment, liberties, privileges and rights which the colored laborers never dream of obtaining. When white laborers take hold of the Southland, then you will see the laborers in the saddles and the employers on foot. Then will come socialism, anarchy and all the evils which necessarily follow."

It is politics first, politics last and politics all the time which brings about the race disturbances. If there is to be a conflict, it must be a conflict brought on entirely by the whites. No considerable number of Negroes dream of causing any unpleasantness, much less do they talk about it. The white men certainly will not attack the blacks anyhow, notwithstanding these blacks continually cry peace. For as I said to the governor, the lawmakers and the great body of good citizens in Georgia belonging to the Anglo-Saxon race in my open letter. What honor, what glory is derived from a man whipping a babe? How many laurels will crown the brow of the warrior who only fights puny women and undeveloped children? It may be that the women are quarrelsome at times and the children annoying, still the strong, muscular man must understand that neither the one nor the other can be considered, when hostilities are declared, his equal. Such is the case with the great body of my people they are weak while you are strong. They are poor while you are rich, they are young in experience while you are old; they are disorganized while you are organized, and in fact they are so small in comparison to your size that

really to attack them is to make every man who believes
in fair play say "for shame, that they do not fight their
equals."

It is said that the Negro is anxious to loose his black
skin, becoming white; that his school teaches him to
despise himself; that he longs for the association and the
society of the white people in proportion to the numbers
educated; that he wants to miscegenate. Some go so
far as to say that certain would-be respectable colleges
make the race question a serious problem by teaching
that the only solution is amalgamation—the blacks and
the whites intermarrying; and in this way, in the future,
making only one race—a mongrel—in this country. Such
a thing will never be. In fact, intermixing of races will
not take place any oftener than murders, robberies and
other grave crimes which are legislated against. This
world is not inhabited by angels, and the fools are not all
dead. What I said some time ago about this intermixing
of races by intermarriage I say again. As for amalgamation, you need not fear that. Race wholeness and race
integrity will be maintained without laws being enacted to
have it so. This is said without any desire to reflect un-
pleasantly on those States enjoying a law preventing
intermarriage. As long as crows follow crows, geese
follow geese, coal with coal, gold with gold; plants of a
kind each in their own clime and locality, you need have
no fears that the human family will become less distinct-
ive. God enjoys variety, and he will always force the
best in each race to care more for its own particular
kind than for another's.

It is a subject for congratulation that colored men, as
well as those of the other race, are studying this "race
question" or problem. Eminent gentlemen, like Dr.
Boggs, Governor Lee, Senator Ingalls, Hon Henry
W Grady and Dr. Curry seem to think that the question
or subject is a problem. In fact, seven-eighths of the
"great minds" of the country decide that it is a problem so
complicated and intricate that no statesman has, as yet,
been found able to give a satisfactory solution. Mr
John T Shufton and a few others to be found in
both races, including the writer, are helplessly in the
minority. And whether or not we would call the subject
a "problem," we must at least admit that the subject is

one of growing interest. In an interview or communication published in the *New York World*, November 5th. 1889. Mr Shufton, who is a Negro lawyer and author in Orlando, Florida, says "The situation down here needs no solution, for it is not a problem There are three distinct causes of irritation and disturbance at the South. These are political, social and moral, and the first is a greater source of evil than all the others combined There can be no satisfactory adjustment, no permanent peace between the two races at the South until the Negro abandons politics and bids farewell to political glory in these States A persistent effort on the part of the Negro to attain that which he never can attain, will inevitably lead to conflict, the horrors of which are unimaginable. It is this relentless persistency on the part of the one race to be, and the relentless persistency on the part of the other to prevent it from being—and prevent it they will at all cost—that causes the trouble" The gentleman from whom we quote can never expect perpetual peace, if it is to be obtained in the way he maps out No Democratic leader of sound sense and judgment is guilty of asking such a settlement. It is impossible to do what Mr Shufton says entirely Education makes men ambitious The crudite mind desires to impress itself on some individual, and that "mind will do so or kill the man that carries it. Gentlemen will learn that the thing finally to be worshipped is not "matter," but "mind." As long as the school-houses dot the hills, the Negro colleges adorn the States of the South and a respectable number of Negroes pay taxes just so long will there be a cry by colored men for representation Not a cry for controlling power, not a cry to dominate and rule the white people, but a cry to say something about their "own affairs," their "own interests" in the halls of legislation, school boards and city councils It is said that if the colored people would proceed about getting described recognition properly, it would not cause offence to the ruling powers of this section

But be that as it may. no sensible white man will ever expect the colored people, on their own motion, to go out of politics The white man does not ask that they should· he does ask that when recognition is sought of, that it shall be by the best colored men, and shall be solicited at their hands, and not at the hands of those persons of the white race who have done so much to estrange the races and separate, by a distinct line, this section from the North   I have never known a respectable committee of colored men to ask in a respectful manner for a favor from the rulers of the South but what it was instantly granted   The thing the white men South will never quietly submit to is the forced recognition of the Negro for political place among them   On the other hand, I believe the South is quite willing to grant minority representation to the Negro in every Southern State. Negroes have been elected to the legislature. They have been seated, appointed on committees and given the same recognition and enjoyed the same courtesies as other members   In the courts they are treated with the utmost kindness, and so far as treatment is concerned, the only distinction which is made the Negro makes it himself.

It is said that the Negro's idea of first-class is to be with "white folks;" that if the white people all rode in the smoking car, and he was given a seat in the parlor coach, he would feel uncomfortable and complain of being proscribed, interdicted, discriminated against, and given second-class   I hope the statement does not reflect the condition of the majority of the race, but I am afraid it does   The Negro has been trained to look up to the white man and to regard him as the owner and enjoyer of the "best" there is in the land, so, if he mistakes second-class, when accepted by a white man to be first-class, I am not surprised   The talk of a conflict between the races is talk for nothing. The two races here are bound together by many ties   I had occasion to say in my "open letter," on the question of extermination, a few things which may sound coarse, but which I originally presented in the most friendly spirit, and which I reproduce here, with a heart filled with genuine affection for both races. Morpheus takes me into sleep, at night, while I am thinking that, somewhere in the wide range of God's mercy, God's justice and God's love, all men will be' housed from the storm and everlastingly saved   To live, feeling this way, and to die the same, ought to be happiness enough for any one. On the question I said " As for extermination, that will never take place   First, because

500 Negro babies are born every day. Second, because not only is the colored man's prolificness increasing the blacks in this country, but because members of every nationality belonging to your great race are helping him to produce a dark population, by maintaining a sinful relation with females of his race. Third, because blood is thicker than water, and while this statement may be unpleasant it is nevertheless true. The sons and daughters, nephews and nieces, aunts and uncles, who, while belonging to the black race, find their close kinsmen among white people will never be exterminated. Their white relatives are too noble and brave to destroy the fruit of their indulgences. Again, there are relations other than these which declare that the races are here to remain, and after a while it will be found that "the whites are getting whiter, while the blacks are getting blacker." Since the colored man cannot be amalgamated or exterminated, what shall be done with him? What is the proper course to be pursued? Can he be colonized? Will you send him to the Northwest? Or will you by deportation place him in Africa, a country from which his forefather came? Shall the Negro emigrate? Is the Negro a success as an immigrant? What does the Liberian experiment teach? These are questions which must be answered before a start is made for other fields. Can this country get along without the Negro, and be as happy and as prosperous as now? Is not the Negro a better subject for citizenship than the foreigner? Does not the fact that the Negro was born and reared here make him, necessarily, more of a patriot and more in love with American institutions than the foreigner, born and reared up under a monarchical form of government, coming here only because he is poor and wants to make money? Is there not more of a problem around the doings of the anarchist, the socialist and Castle Garden than there is around the black people of this country, described by Gov. Hill, as being "untutored, superstitious and helpless but patient, docile and ambitious?" A conflict there must never be. The two races, placed here together by God must continue throughout the ages, their relation of interdependence, in peace, recognizing as the only distinction between them that one is in white and must therefore socially associate with whites while the other is in black.

and must, necessarily, mingle with blacks.   Birds of a
feather, birds of a kind, flock together.

CHAPTER V

SHALL THE WHITE MAN AND THE NEGRO SEPARATE?

No   A thousand times no   The white man is sure to
stay here, and as for the colored man, he is not only
unwilling to go away, but he is unable to emigrate.   It is
impossible to separate the races, and time consumed in
discussing the advisability of separation is time lost
There will never be a time when all the white people
will be in one country and all the black people will be in
another   There may be a time when there will be such
an arrangement perfected, as will allow a portion of one
race to separate from the country peopled by both, but
such a thing as treeing the United States of Negroes or
white people entirely can never be accomplished.   Certain persons will, of course, from time to time, elect to
leave the United States, but there will be no sending of
persons, white or black, out of the country by force of
legislation

In my talk with a newspaper man, the following was
said in answer to the question   "What do you think of
colonizing the Negroes?"

Where are you going to send them?   There is no
place worth having, from a money and health standpoint,
but what is already partly occupied by white people   Of
course there is no such thing as legislating the colored
people out of the country until there has been a repeal
of the fifteenth amendment to the Constitution.   Until
that is done, it is foolish to even talk about colonizing my
race, for the government, under the present law, can
appropriate no money for such a purpose, and because
at present we are full fledged citizens, and can do as we
please about going or staying

I must confess, that I was disgusted, when I heard that
a number of Negro preachers, of the Baptist denomina-
tion, had passed resolutions, asking the government for
fifty million dollars for colonization purposes.   I have
regarded the leading men of the Baptist church as being

very learned, but this action does not increase my regard
and respect for them, as thinkers It may be that
" smarting " with wounded feelings and bleeding backs,
received and caused in connection with the Baxley outrage, prevented that calm and considerate deliberation
which usually characterizes their meetings. Anyhow,
the passing of such resolutions as were passed, and the
incendiary speeches which were made in their convention, gives another proof of what men will do while filled
with angry passion Instead of memorializing Congress
and the President of the United States, they ought to
have gone into Georgia and laid their grievances before
a grand jury, had the parties committing the outrage
indicted, tried and convicted. They ought, also, to have
taken action against the East Tennessee Railroad for
damages, and not refrained from doing so on account
of that road, by its agent pretending to be sorry for the
occurrence, and probably distributing tickets or passes
freely among them. But they say: " It is the policy of
the State to keep the races separate on the cars, having
coaches equal in accommodation for each." That is
true, but if you were put into a certain car, by an agent
of that company, and the conductor countenanced the
unlawful attack of those men, the outragers, the railroad company was liable. "But we cannot get justice
in a Georgia court " How do you know ? Go into the
courts and see what they will do. Hire able and fear-
less attorneys, there are plenty of them in Georgia, and
appeal to your home people for redress and not to strangers Keep a correct and accurate minute of the testi-
mony, and if the jury, according to your prejudiced
expectation, find a verdict in favor of the defendants, pub-
lish thousands of copies of the whole proceedings, evidence, speeches, charge of the court and verdict, let a
copy, if possible, find its way into every home, and the
sense of right and justice, which are in the majority in
this country—the South, will, in the end, give you the
victory But no, you take the wrong position, you act
as though you would have the men of this section, who
have a freedom equaling that found in Maine, forced into
doing, by Northern interference, that which you want done,
but which you have never asked the men here, in the
right way, to do Commence and do your first work

over. Every land has a remedy for its own ills All
Negro "meetings," before adjournment, take on a political complexion, and that. of course, makes the petitions
coming from said "meetings," offensive to the rulers of
the South. It appears that politics is made a business,
paramount to everything else. This is wrong. While
no one, of proper intelligence, demands that you shall
stop taking a part in politics, it is thought best that you
should regard politics as an incident, and not as the only
occupation requiring attention

The thing which injures the colored people most is
the stress which they place on politics as a panacea for
all their ills. Less politics and more land is what the
Negro wants.

Stay here Go to work and learn well your duties as
citizens Mr. Ellis. a colored man from Texas, now in
Mexico, in the interest of a few deceived, deluded blacks,
has succeeded in having the law-makers of that Republic sanction, by legislative enactment, the coming of
Negroes from the United States among them, provided
they will live in that part of Mexico unfit for Mexican
settlement On the twenty-second day of November,
the following "associated press" dispatch appeared in all
the large papers of the United States

"Mexican newspapers state that Negro colonists will
only be permitted to settle in fever districts on the coast '

Stay here; this is your country as well as the white
man's: cultivate and maintain an amicable relation with
the people of this section Do nothing which will
destroy amity; have a proper regard for the rights of
others. and you will never have cause to complain because
your next door neighbor is a white man

As to whether you shall go to Africa or stay here, I
reproduce my interview with an Atlanta Constitution
reporter, published December 31. 1887. I understand
Dr. E. W. Blyden, a West Indian linguist, is now in this
country. He is challenged to meet me in public debate.
if he cares to. and prove false my assertions. He is
here, by the grace of God, although the Liberians led
him through the streets of Monrovia with a rope around
his neck, for a cause, as I am informed, which I do not
care to mention Liberia is Latrobe's and Coppinger's
graveyard, set apart for the destruction and burial of

American Negroes I have read of no penitentiary in this country, but what is preferable to "The Black Republic." if the question of character is waived The Colonization Society, in Washington, should be abated as an aggravated nuisance There should be a law passed in each State, saying· Any man found telling or encouraging Negroes to go to that part of Africa where Liberia is situated, shall, upon conviction, be declared a felon, and imprisoned in the State's prison, for not less than one year nor more than ten, in the discretion of the trial judge Provided that, if the defence is insanity, it shall be taken as established, and the court shall have power, and it is made the duty of the court, to have the prisoner locked up, where he can do no harm Here is the talk I had with the reporter, before my term of office as U. S Minister and Consul-General expired

"Tell me about Liberia," said the reporter

"Liberia is a small place to talk so much about, but there is much that I can tell, and a great deal more that I can't tell you until after the twelfth of January. Until that time diplomatic receive will prevent me "

"Oh, I don't want any state secrets," said the reporter "Just the country and the people Is it so that you are disgusted with the country ?"

"Well, let me explain that There are twelve thousand 'civilized' people—people who have been sent from this country, and 988,000 natives Now I am heartily disgusted with the twelve thousand 'civilized' people, and I am very much pleased with the 988,000 natives—the heathens, you understand. The natives are superior to the American negroes mentally, physically, and morally I say that they are superior morally, though the Americans are 'Christians,' and the natives are heathens It is a fact The Americans are cheats, they preach and convert nobody—they pray and get rich off of the natives Twenty-two thousand people have been sent from this country in the last sixty-six years, and yet to-day there are only 12,000 'civilized' people and 2,375 voters It is just this way. The 12,000 survivors of the 22,000 emigrants are virtually slave owners, and are settled along the coast. The tribes in contact with them have adopted the vices of the new-comers, without their virtues, and are really slaves to the 12,000 But nine-tenths of the

natives are practically independent of the Liberian government."

"What does the country look like?"

"Liberia is a low, swampy country. The soil is won-
derfully fertile, and the country is rich in ores—gold, silver, iron and copper. The choicest woods in the world,
mahogany, ebony, *lignumvitæ* and scores of others are
found in wonderful abundance."

"Are any of the resources being developed?"

"Not one. There are no mines, no roads even that
extend over half a mile from any town. Even agriculture
is in its most primitive form. They have only five plows
in Liberia. They have a bill-hook with a flat point, and
they tickle the earth with that, and the harvests are wonderful. Why, a fellow digs with the same bill-hook that
his great-grandfather used. There are no mules, no cows,
no horses The transporting is done on the heads and
shoulders of the men and women."

"How large is the country?"

"It lies between 7° 4′ and 3° 20′ north latitude Bounded
on the north by the British province, Sierra Leone, and
on the south by the French province of Lagos. The
stretch of sea coast is about two hundred and sixty miles,
and from the ocean it extends indefinitely into the center
—say from two hundred to three hundred miles."

"I suppose the country is modelled, as far as practicable, after the United States?"

"Yes, the country is divided into four provinces, cor-
responding to States. They are called 'counties,' and in
the order of importance are Montserrado, Bassah, Sinoe
and Maryland. There is a senate of eight members, a
house of representatives of thirteen members, and the
rest of the national officers, of which there are in all 1,-
333, from the cabinet to the bailiffs, are appointed by the
president. The president, the senate, the representatives and the mayors of the towns are elected by the 2,-
375 voters. Just think, 1,333 officers out of 2,375 voters.
It is a fact that every voter in the country is holding, or
has held, one or more offices They have a Secretary of
War, but only one regiment. The flower of the army is
the Johnson Guards, named in honor of the present president. There are in that company seventeen officers
and two privates, and the privates insist on walking by

themselves Then there are the Newport Guards, named after Mary Newport, the heroine of Liberia, who fired the first gun against the rebels in the last insurrection. The officers are promised, on an average, $6 50 per month They get about $4.85 per year, if they get anything You understand, though, that English money is almost the only money used. You might say that trade is all barter. Money is very little used."

"Well, how does the country hang together?"

"It don't 'hang together' always The natives acknowledge a vague sort of submission to the president of Liberia, because it is convenient to go to Monrovia and exchange their palm oil and gold dust for cloth and hats and kettles. But occasionally they frail out the government. The last insurrection cost Liberia $7,000 The Vey people killed two Liberians, and the government troops fled in frantic confusion without even returning the fire There was another insurrection which cost the government $4,000. That was Cape Palmas. The government had purchased a lot of cannons from the United States, and when the insurgents fired the Liberians ran, though not a soul was killed The cannons fell into the hands of the insurgents But it is convenient, you see, to acknowledge the president, and most of them do so as long as he lets them alone."

"The government troops don't amount to much then?"

"No, they do not. The captain of the Johnson Guards wears a plug hat and an umbrella. The men are at liberty to wear just what they please, and they drill for hours with a slave or two behind each man to hold his gun They hunt that way, too The 'apprentices' go behind and 'tote' the gun till the master gets ready to fire it off "

"What about education?"

"The missionary societies of New York and Boston used to have some missions. There was also a Liberian college, but this is defunct. The schools are exceedingly few and weak, and used only by the 12,000, or rather by a very few of that 12,000 "

"What about society?"

"How do you mean? Prejudice? Well, I should say there is more prejudice in Liberia between the Americans and various classes of natives than there is in the

United States between white and black. There is infi-
nitely more. A native is not allowed to enter by the front
door of the 'civilized' man's house The native children
are not allowed to enter the schools, nor to strike the child
of a civilized man under any circumstances whatever
The only connection that the natives have with the church
is when they go to carry prayer books or umbrellas
for their masters, and sit on the doorstep and sleep in the
sunshine until the sermon is over. You have no idea how
many castes there are, and how sharply they are defined."

"And religion?"

"Lots of it, lots of it I boarded with a civilized man
who had three children and a wife. The man belonged
to one church, the wife to another, and each of the three
children to a different one. Why? 'Oh,' he said, 'when
the societies send over good things we can get some of
all.' That father had only one regret. and that was that he
had no more children. And collections. Why a man
with a hundred dollars and who knew how to play poker
could break the republic in two nights "

"And the native religion?"

"That's pretty. The girls are kept in the 'gregory-bush'
until they are seventeen, and the boys in the 'devil-bush'
until they are eighteen. The boys wear a gauze cap which
they remove under no consideration until they leave
the 'bush.' On that they are taught their honor, virtue and
life depend, and if the cap is removed all this is lost The
girls wear a charm around their necks, and this answers
precisely to the caps worn by the boys. The young people are remarkably chaste They wear no clothing, and
mingle freely, but only where the natives have come in
contact with the civilized are ever found instances of
unchastity. The natives also are truthful, honest and intelligent The Veys are the most powerful native tribe
and are brown, not black They are the best formed I
have ever seen. Some of the women are remarkably
pretty. I never saw a dwarf or an idiot among them
They believe in a hereafter, and in a supreme being
called 'Cumbah.' But 'Cumbah' has a wife and children,
and is very much like a god of Roman or Greek antiq-
uity. He is very much like a mortal, and much more
intelligible to them than a Great Spirit who has a Son but
no wife, and the Holy Ghost is something they can't con-

ceive The idea of three persons in one is the same way Then take into consideration the cheating and brutality of the 'civilized' people, and you cannot wonder that they prefer their own religion "

"Polygamists ?"

"Oh, yes it is different from the Utah polygamy, and much prettier When a man dies his wives are taken by his brother A young woman has no choice whatever as to the man she shall marry. With the young fellow it is different His parents choose his first wife for him She remains th 'head wife' ever after The parents are very careful, and the son never thinks of objecting. The male parent, of course, has most to say about the son's marriage, but the mother is also allowed a voice They together make a choice By the way, the boy tells his mother that he wishes to marry, and she tells the father. After the choice is made, they bargain for the girl The first payment, if the bargain is made is a string of beads This clinches the bargain It is a sort of instrument sale as it were Divorce ? No the natives have no divorce The civilized people have The president has been three times divorced It is terribly common amongst the civilized "

"What about woman's position ? "

"Woman is a kind of property They have no vote, though I am sure they would govern better than the men They are more intelligent They live to an almost incredible age It is very common, indeed to find persons considerably over one hundred years old The reason Mary Newport came to be so prominent is this Whenever there is a popular hue-and-cry—when there is frenzy of any kind, the women are invariably leaders. Why, two of the presidents have been killed by the populace, not assassinated, but actually mobbed

'What about the climate ?'

"Wet six months, dry six months I have seen it rain for two weeks without stopping ten minutes aggregate stop in the whole time It pours, too, when it does rain "

"Tell me something about the native marriage ceremony."

"That's a queer thing The boy, you remember leaves the 'devil-bush' at eighteen He is then initiated into

what h, s before been a secret, by two old men The girl
has not   The girl is brought in and placed on a mat. He
is brought in blindfolded.   The bandage is removed from
his eyes, he sees his future wife, smiles, and is led out.
Then the celebrating, feasting, and dancing begins
There is no further ceremony   Now, when a chief's son
marries a chief's daughter. the ceremony takes two weeks
instead of a few minutes.   The parties meet midway between the two homes, no matter what the distance.   The
woman's foot is not allowed to touch the ground   Skins
and cloths are spread before her, taken up after she has
passed, and again spread in her path "

"Well, what sort of provision does the young fellow
make before he takes a wife ?"

"No man can have a wife unless he can provide for her.
A village is built in a circle, and all the houses are one.
The roofs are thatched together.   Not only the houses
but everything else is in common   As long as one Koo-
man has rice, his tribe has rice   The ground in the
center is the dance ground, and the villagers dance at
every sunset   The plagues are the 'bugga-buggas,' or
white ants, led by a queen   Then there are the 'drivers,'
with their generals, colonels, captains and privates, all
of different sizes, and having different degrees of author-
ity.   They are the scavengers. Just you spill palm oil, or
'et your floor get filthy, and here they come by millions and
millions. They surround a house, forming a ring eighteen
inches thick, all matted and interlocked so that if you put a
cane under the ring and lift it, it would not break, but
would rise like a rubber belt for ten feet on each side.
You can tell what's in your house when they come.
After the ring has been formed, a lizard spies them
He rushes frantically about, convinces himself that they
are really 'drivers,' and he drops to the floor, and does
not attempt to escape, and offers no resistance   Then
you see lizards, serpents, scorpions by the hundred. All
drop. The 'drivers' eat everything but gold, silver and
iron   The 'bugga-buggas' take a table leg, for example,
eat the center, leaving the shell   If they happen to visit
your house when every one is away, you might suspect
nothing until you leaned against the side of the house or
pushed the door, and the thing would collapse in a little
heap—a shell."

"What makes a wealthy native?"

"Brass kettles and women Old Too-glass is chief of the Kroo people, and the wealthiest man near Liberia, because he has most women and most brass kettles."

"What are the relations of Liberia to this government?"

Liberia is an independent farce It is in no way dependent on the United States I tell you what they ought to do The United States government ought to claim Liberia as a dependency —no European country could object Then appoint a governor Pay the government officials, and develop that country. They ought to send a revenue cutter or two over there, and enforce the laws. The revenue at present $83,000 annually could be easily raised to $1,000,000 —which would more than defray government expenses The Monroe doctrine don't apply Then with the United States to back them, syndicates could be formed, commerce would prosper amazingly, and the wonderful mines and forests would bountifully repay all effort"

"But you don't believe in sending Negroes there?"

"No, sir Africans must develop Africa Organize them and they will accomplish wonders. Encourage and sustain them, and they will develop Liberia"

The scope of this little book will not permit a more extended review of that dark, disagreeable and death giving country Stay here! black men and white men, born on American soil. Put restrictions which will amount to absolute prohibition on Castle Garden Keep the foreigners, with their anarchistic ideas out of America, and save this country for the happiness and prosperity of the true sons of the soil. But if the experiment must be tried of Negro colonization which I honestly think wholly unnecessary, adopt the plan marked out in my reply to "An Appeal to Pharaoh." Here is the proposition On account of the fact that in 1880, there were in South Carolina, 391,105 white persons and 604,332 Negroes, in Mississippi, 577,308 whites and 650,291 blacks; in Louisiana, 454,954 whites and 483,655 Africans, let these States be given to the Negroes, if you want to see how they will self govern Of course you must first remove "constitutional obstructions" before anything can be lawfully done in the matter. After the legal way has been prepared, let Congress reimburse the whites for the

property they own in the three States mentioned, and
turn these States over to the colored people, allowing
them to carry on the government as now; these States
remaining a part of the Union in the same way that the
others are, with the one exception that the Negroes who
desire to vote or hold office must live in one of the States
mentioned, and the white men desiring to vote or hold
office, must seek and make their residence in other than
the three mentioned States.   Under this system no one
would be "forced" out of a State that did not desire to
leave: on the other hand the extra inducement and inhi-
bition in certain States would necessarily separate the
two noisy elements of this country—the white and the
Negro politician.   This arrangement would also give
the Negro a chance to copy after the white man who is
versed in statecraft.   Again, you can empty the States
mentioned of white men easier than you can of black
men, because the whites do not equal the blacks in number, and because, from a financial standpoint, the whites
are better able to travel   Do this if separation must
take place, thus enabling the separated to make annual
visits to their parents' graves and to the old plantation
where they spent their childhood days   I am of the
opinion that the white people living in the States mentioned will never accept the "proposition" above stated.
It is not necessary that they should, for the once slave
and the once bondsman s descendant, free, a citizen and
enfranchised, can obtain all which equity, justice and
good conscience demand, without any such "going in"
and "coming out" of States long settled and now quietly
enjoying prosperity.   This section—the South—furnishes
homes for two races as distinct as they are inseparable

CHAPTER VI

SHALL THE NEGRO BE DISFRANCHISED ?

That is, shall the Negro be deprived of suffrage?   It is
necessary, before answering this question, that the chapter
on the Negro as a citizen and as a voter be again read
or recalled to your memory   A republic insists on having enlightened citizens, persons who know enough to

select intelligently their law-makers and rulers, each individual being a free and independent man voting con-
scientiously as he pleases and as he thinks is to his best
interest and to the best interest of the community in
which he lives without being hampered by outside interference. Is the colored man, at the present time, such a
voter? Absolute monarchies are the homes prepared for
the ignorant masses. One man there having sufficient
power physically as soldier, and intellectually as statesman to fight his way to the Czar's "height" or the emperor's eminence, and from that position deal out such
justice and make such rules as he pleases. There is only
one "mind" in an absolute monarchy. In a republic it is intended that each member thereof shall possess a "mind."
For the founders of the republic declared, in unmistakable
words, "all men are created free and equal (in a
republic), with certain unalienable rights, and that among
these are life, liberty and the pursuit of happiness." If
the colored voters, who, so far as the law can make them,
are clothed with the same privileges as the white voters,
intend to continue voting as though one head was enough
for the more than eight millions, as though they were
not expected to read the 'platform' of political parties, to
study the "personnel" of the ticket, to investigate the im-
portant questions agitating the public mind; if they must
always think of before the war times and the "we freed you
cry;" if they must be unforgiving and relentless in their hate
against those who now employ them and who once owned
a number of them; if they intend that this hatred shall extend against the white man here and his children, even
unto the third and fourth generation; if there is always to
be political war; if these black voters mean to refuse
the olive branch of political peace offered by Grover
Cleveland, as the leader of Democracy; if they are going
to remain solid always, never dividing, notwithstanding
white men made all the parties in existence, and have,
with their intelligence, themselves divided and made six
or seven different political parties; if the conduct of the
Negro is to be so united and solid in their voting strength,
bringing down on themselves the curses of political op-
ponents and the contempt of those whom they take as
political friends, then by all means disfranchise them, and
that speedily. Take away from the Negro the "ballot"

which, as used heretofore by him, served only to make voting a farce and the republic a mockery, so far as having enlightened black citizens, understanding the responsibility of citizenship. That this argument, made as an appeal for a division of the Negro vote between the political parties, will be resisted by a number of honorable men I have no doubt. To my statement now made that no other nationality votes solidly one ticket, will come the reply, that no other class of people are situated as are the Negroes. To the statement that the Negroes are divided in church belief, in society preference, and differ in taste, in physical appearance and in every way except politically, comes the answer that they are kept in one party by a "condition which confronts them," other parties refusing to accept them on equal footing as members, and on account of no recognition being given them by the dominant party in the South, in the way of dividing the offices, affording the black voters, as a respectable part of the South, minority representation.

The reason colored men are not accepted readily into the Democratic party is because, as a rule, they make a condition of their coming "receiving something," office or other thing of value. They say I am a Democrat in one breath and ask for office or money in the next. This has been carried on so long until the Democratic party has no confidence in the Negro as a patriotic, loyal member of its party. They have learned by many painful, practical lessons of experience that the Negro loves the Republican party as he loves his soul, and that, except in rare cases, he only votes against that party out of revenge or for the hope of reward, in money or its equivalent. The Negro must start first—not the white man of the South—for it is the Negro who stands most in need. It is your duty to restore confidence in the Southern white man, by teaching him by your overt acts that you can be honest, loyal and consistent in other than the Republican party. But you, as colored voters, say, "how can we leave the Grand Old Party, which Mr. Douglass calls 'The ship, all else the sea,' in the face of outrages being daily committed upon our race?" There are foul and devilish outrages committed in the South which will not be lightly passed over. The good white men of this section regret these occurrences, these outbreaks, and if the good colored men, instead of murmuring and flaunting the red flag in the face of the ruling whites, who want law and order observed, by sending reports North, worded in such a way as to indicate that everybody here endorsed the outrages, would join in helping to apprehend and bring to justice these violators of law, order would be more easily maintained. The colored people South must learn to obey law and to help in its enforcement, and they must be as anxious to see a Negro criminal brought to justice as a white man violating the law. Then it would be well to remember that outrages are occurring as frequently in the North as in the South. When the statistics are gathered it will be found that there are fifty cases of conflicts within each race, both parties to it being black, or both parties to it being white, to every conflict between men of the two races.

This talk of outrage is greatly exaggerated for political effect. The Democratic party does not live by reason of many Democrats having owned slaves, by reason of many men who vote the Democratic ticket being charged with committing outrages. The Democratic party disclaims a desire for the return of the former, denounces in strong terms the latter, and still lives in spite of the fact that both are true. The sensible Negroes are natural Democrats if they only understood themselves. They believe in decentralization as against centralization, they all are in favor of the greatest amount of liberty to the individual consistent with the well-being of society, they are opposed to sumptuary and class legislation: they believe in the greatest good to the greatest number, they want the government economically administered; the war taxes taken off, the purchasing capacity of the dollar increased, and a tariff so adjusted as to pay the expenses of the government only.

Prejudice, and prejudice alone, is what keeps many of them from voting as I have indicated, and fear of social ostracism from those of their race who are not quite as far advanced. Let them be liberalized and made conservative.

Let the colored tax-payers and the white tax-payers, both possessing intelligence, get together, and let each swear eternal friendship for the other. Let them build

up a fence high, and make it so secure that the worthless
political demagogue, owning nothing and having no
calling except that of the breeder of dissension and
strife, cannot get over or through it Let the colored
voter decide that there are men enough in the South,
born here, to hold all the offices, and vote accordingly.
Vote on, being governed by the rule that your interests
are identical with your white neighbors, and that you are
not only physically but politically free as well Vote in
the way indicated, and as a free and honest citizen, and
as an intelligent handler of the "ballot," you will be
regarded as a blessing in the community where you
reside. The man who will sell his vote ought to be
from that day forever disfranchised. The man who will
purchase a vote should thenceforth be disqualified from
holding office True citizenship, with the right to vote,
is that which gives the individual enjoying the same the
right to take part in the legislative and judicial proceedings of the community, and requires of him the
carrying of an equal share of the community's burdens
and responsibilities

CHAPTER VII

OUR CHRISTIAN DUTY

Since both races are here to stay never to be separated,
let us come to some understanding and agreement with
each other In treating as to terms remember that there
are two sides to the subject and agreement: and that
there are two races equally interested in the final setttle-
ment or the terms of the " peace arrangement " Colored men on account of the " wrong doing" of a few
white men do not consider all white men bad: therefore
white men should not, because one Negro steals, say all
Negroes are thieves. There are good and noble men in
both races in the South Men who despise " wrong
doing" of every kind I know white men of this section
that I would trust with any interest which I hold dear
Who could imagine or picture General J B. Gordon, Editor Henry W Grady, Mayor John T. Glenn, Captain
Harry Jackson, Lawyer Hoke Smith, or men of their

class and rank, unwilling and refusing to measure out full justice to the once oppressed race? These gentlemen stand ready to grant, when properly asked, every just right to which the Negro in Georgia is entitled. And progressive men like these can be found in every State in the South, ready and willing to prove by tangible evidence to the world that they are the best friends of the black men. These men take no delight in reading of attacks made on Negroes. All they ask is to be allowed to settle the Southern question for themselves. They rightly claim that living here, they understand the situation better than persons who know only of the "present South" by what they read in the newspapers. Under the present policy of the South, the colored people have been able to acquire one hundred and seventy-five million dollars worth of property, and although the colored people are not given as yet recognition in the distribution of State and municipal offices, there is every reason why they should feel encouraged. A number of colored men have been educated as doctors and lawyers by white physicians and white barristers of the South. These professional Negroes have hung out their shingles, and where they once moved as slaves, they now live as successful practitioners. In treatment they are accorded the same attention, courtesy and kindness extended to white men of the same calling. This is certainly a long distance to travel in twenty-four years. College professors, mechanics, tradesmen, bishops and theologians all over the South with black faces. In Washington, Wilkes county, the home of Hon Robert Toombs, a carriage is sent with a committee of white men to escort a Negro Bishop, Rt Rev W J. Gaines, to the largest church for white people in the city, to preach to white people about the "Unspeakable riches of God's kingdom reserved for the Saints." In Milledgeville every white church in the city is given up during the A M E Conference to the colored preachers, and not only the churches but the opera house. Did these Negroes surrender their manhood to obtain these things? No. They simply conducted themselves like sober, conservative, Christian gentlemen, and were treated accordingly. The court rooms, the State capitols and the opera houses throughout the South are given to the colored people, in which to hold their meetings and conventions from time to time. Are not these evidences of the fact that the South is rapidly going forward and losing sight of prejudice? The Southern white men will give the Negro all he merits. The Atlanta *Journal* has repeatedly called the attention of the railroad companies to the distinction made in providing for colored accommodation at the depots, and in the cars prepared for their conveyance. This paper is not alone Only a few days ago the Charleston *News and Courier* "hauled" the railroads "over the coals" for a failure to provide equal accommodation for their colored passengers

All over the South, regardless of the Negro "hot heads" and the white "kickers," a sentiment is present, and on the increase, which is gradually clothing the Negro with responsibilities in proportion to the number answering to the standard by which they are measured, to-wit. Intellectual, financial and moral fitness—more stress being put on the first and last than on the other In mentioning a few things which ought to be granted, I deny a disposition to lecture anybody, to refuse to be thankful for what has been and is being done, or to appear offensive and dictatorial. What I say is for the good of the whole country, and I trust I am actuated by the purest motives If in this world I have an enemy, he is unknown to me ; that my heart is friendly to all is proven by a reiteration of an earnest expression of mine which appeared in print some time ago. It was " No man loves his race more than I love mine. It may be that I shall die misunderstood, just as I have lived misrepresented ; suffer me to say that, so great is my love for the race to which I belong, I stand ready, if such a thing be possible, to remain the balance of my life, however long, in any prison, however vile, to perpetuate peace between the sons of Japheth and the sons of Ham." I am ready at any day to keep my word Be at peace with God, knowing that you have treated your neighbor right, and there is no more pleasant death than dying for your country.

Concerning the Negro, decide without debate that you brought him here in his parents from Africa, not at his request, certainly without his consent Then decide that you taught him all he knows about your

civilization as well as your religion and customs If you
find he is making an apt pupil, do not become angry, but
be consoled by remembering that you teach, that life is
always progress and that man never attains the end ; if
this be true, and if intellectually you are the peer of the
Negro, (and it is said you are superior,) considering the
start you had when the Negro began, you will be quite
able to keep the same distance ahead.   It is not believed
that your race will tire of work   Your race is from a
zone of industry : mine from a hot belt, where rest is
always desirable.   Decide that, in the operation of
the laws, everywhere in the South the Negro shall
have full justice: that criminals among us shall be punished, while the innocent shall go free, that the sober
and industrious shall be righteously compensated, while
the intemperate and lazy shall find their bed filled with
thorns.   Decide that the Negro race must be judged not
by the standard of a people who have been actively engaged as masters of the world for centuries, but by the
heights to which they have reached, considering the
depths from which they emerged, about twenty-five years
ago   Decide that we have men who are bad among us,
and very bad, and that the same is true of every race which
God has made.   Give to the colored man in this country
the justice which you would like to have if you were in
Africa, and which I would contend you should have, did
I reside there, during your stay.   Shall the Negro be
more just than the white man ? Shall he be more
polite ? Decide that, as far as practicable, the colored
race shall have the right of conducting and controlling
their own affairs   Encourage them to be self-reliant,
teaching them always that lengthened dependence emas-
culates   Decide that the best colored citizens shall be
treated in keeping with their conduct, and not subjected
to the coarse treatment dished out to those who would
fail to appreciate treatment of another sort.   Lift the
black man up, make him morally, intellectually and in-
dustrially whatever he is susceptible of being made   he
is the best friend you have, and will always be, if you
will let him   His desire for office and prominence he
learned from you   It is well understood that the varie-
gated Negro race, in part educated, is different to the
Negro race of *ante bellum* days   All this is a natural

outgrowth of a changed condition, to some extent
changed surrroundings and changed association. No
man thanks your race more than I for your past favors
shown. Had you desired you could have made our road
more rough. I admit that fully forty per cent. of our
progress in the last quarter of a century must be sub-
tracted and added to your side of the column in payment
for the copy which you daily place before us We
imitate you in dress, language and acts, and we call your
white God our God, and your heaven our abiding place

I love this Southland ; it is the clime congenial to my
color. I have seen sights in my imagination which
scare me.   I see the superintendent (a dream) of the
U. S. census instructing his subordinates that in taking
the census, not to count the colored people, but simply to
count the white folks. (Since this was originally published, Pledger's convention said, dodge the census taker.)
I also see the succeeding Congress apportioning the
representation in Congress on this new census, and in the
same way the strength of the new electoral college   I
go further, and see that while this practically disfran-
chises the colored race, it reduces the representation in
the national Congress about one-half of what it now is
from the South ; the same affliction falling on the
electoral college, I see as a result a farewell given to
Democrats who are aspirants for the presidency, I see
both "houses" in Washington forever Republican ; I
see fat appropriations going elsewhere for internal im-
provements than South, and one hundred and more fear-
ful sights to this section, all on account of the imprudent
conduct of a few men, who absolutely refuse to see how
the many are injured by having to bear the sins of a few
Now in God's name let steps be taken to unite the good
men of both races, and let these say to the lawless and
unthoughtful that peace shall prevail. Adopt a course
which will assure the dark child of this section that
friendly feeling for him is on the increase. Do not let
him think the opposite.

Remember Ohio, Illinois, Indiana, Michigan, Rhode
Island, Connecticut, Massachusetts and the greatest of all,
New York, are debatable ground, with the Negro divided.
If you would benefit by the division, let them see that you

are indeed caring for the life and property of their black brothers, and that division will speedily come

You gentlemen know if the Negro did not vote in the national elections, you would win the fight from the Republicans easily Seeing that this is true, the only thing that you need to do is to command a cessation of hostilities by the few among your race, who are engaged in such work, and show the Negroes North that you are caring for all the beneficial and material interests of the Negroes South, and a glorious era will dawn upon you. While our schools, our cars and waiting rooms at depots are separate, they should be made equal in facilities and accommodation At least this ought to be done, or the companies, in consideration of the difference in accommodation, should make a reduction in the fare when selling tickets to colored people. I am not surprised that there are separate cars for the two races in this State; for I must admit that each time I have been on the cars in the South, a majority of the colored persons in the colored folk's car appeared to have diligently searched out their most dirty clothes in which to travel This ought not to be It is just as much an affliction on the best colored people to have to ride with such unsightly dressed mortals as it is to your race. These railroad hands, going to their work covered with abominable garments, should still have another car Let us all ask the Giver of every good gift to keep the two races of this section friendly to each other, to keep them disposed to give unto each other full justice in every particular. Grave and heavy are the responsibilities of both races, holding the relation of interdependence, so far as employer and employe are concerned. Do not let bad men influence the one race or the other to do wrong, but let the good men in both races get together There are a great many things which both races can afford to grant to each other without in any way endangering the race relation, the race purity, or the race wholeness of either Agree to make these concessions which will mark both races as being equal to the work given them to do Do not think that hunger for a few offices, which Republicans refuse to give colored men, will be sufficient to divide them politically, in the face of the perpetration of unwarranted acts of violence in this section. The colored man, I believe, will divide when acts prove, in every part of our beautiful Southland, that there is actually no difference in the treatment meted out to citizens in the operation of the laws on account of color. Let it be known that a white man outraging a Negro will be as fearlessly and as earnestly hunted down and punished as in the case of a black man outraging a white person. Let there be no inequality in citizenship and all is well. The men upon whose shoulders depend the well-being of our commonwealth are those who fear God and lead sober, moral lives, from whom are selected our statesmen and our public officers.

Let the eminent white preachers, like Dr. McDonald, Dr. Hawthorne, Dr. Lee, Dr. Carpenter and Dr Cleveland, cry aloud, and spare not, from their pulpits until all is as it should be. In the meantime, let such powerful colored preachers as Bishops Turner, Gaines and Grant, Rev. Carter of Atlanta, Rev. Love of Savannah, Rev. W. J. White of Augusta, Rev. Mason of the M. E. Church, Dr. A. E. P. Alberts and Professor Crogman, Holmes and Fortson tell the colored race from the "sacred desk" and in the colleges, that a conciliatory policy must be pursued; that minorities must persuade majorities; that the weak must make friends with the strong, and that the rabid, fire-eating, dissension-creating and strife-sowing politicians must emigrate. Tell the colored people to stop being moved by passion and emotion but to listen to sense and reason. Tell the Negro to help own the developed cities, industries, banks, insurance companies, railroads and other great enterprises. That until he does help own them the white man will remain in control. Tell them that the Negro who does not work should starve. Oppose on every hand the disposition to make five dollars a week and spend seven Tell them to care less for exhibition and more for real worth Tell them to give the circus and street shows the cold shoulder; to invest the money which they heretofore have been foolishly using in this manner, in buying dirt and in educating themselves and their children. Tell the educated Negroes, with a little money, to still love their mothers' race, and despise the thought which bids them leave a race calling so earnestly for their services. Tell them to be glad that they have learning, and to go among the lowly of their race and lift them up. Tell them to ask for no legislation which does not apply alike to whites and blacks Tell them to stand alone, self-reliant, and show the world what they can do in the world of mind and in the world of matter. Tell them not to ask places because they are black, and not to refuse them because they are colored, but to apply, if at all, on merit. If they can't hoe their own row, "tote their own skillet," they should perish from the face of the earth. I say this as a Negro, proud of the fact that my mother was a black woman It makes me sick to hear Negroes sending up baby appeals as though they were never to grow to manhood whereasing and resolving in halls about their wrongs, when they themselves do more to perpetuate these evils than anybody else I hate to hear a black man asking a white man to do for him what he will not do for himself In order to be consistent I claim that the Negro must not ask white men to accept him into their hotels and other public places, until the Negroes owning barber shops and restaurants have the moral courage to accept their own race into them. I do not by this admit that a black man is any better off because he is admitted to places where white men go If my boy goes to school and is rich in intellectual germs, the fact that no white boy attends that school will not prevent him from learning, all other things being equal; but if my boy is a 'dummy" or a "stick," neither will a white boy sitting in a seat by him make him more susceptible of cultivation What the Negro wants most is race pride He wants to believe that his race—the checker-board race, made up of persons so black that you can't get them blacker, and so white that you can't get them any whiter—together form a boquet, and to him is the prettiest race that Jesus died for. Respect the women of the race, I mean those who have not brought shame upon it No people who have failed to respect their ladies have ever amounted to anything Stop caring for a name. Don't get angry if somebody says you are a Negro instead of a colored man, because you are not colored Black is the absence of color. All colors blended make white. Hereafter the white man must be called the colored man and the heretofore alleged colored man must be called the Negro "A leopard cannot change his spots " I have never